WEST AND EAST YORKSHIRE BUSES AND TROLLEYBUSES IN 1962

T0286936

PHILIP WALLIS

AMBERLEY

First published 2022

Amberley Publishing
The Hill, Stroud
Gloucestershire, GL5 4EP

www.amberley-books.com

Copyright © Philip Wallis, 2022

The right of Philip Wallis to be identified as
the Author of this work has been asserted in
accordance with the Copyrights, Designs and
Patents Act 1988.

ISBN 978 1 3981 0912 4 (print)
ISBN 978 1 3981 0913 1 (ebook)

British Library Cataloguing in Publication Data.
A catalogue record for this book is available from
the British Library.

Typesetting by SJmagic DESIGN SERVICES, India.
Printed in the UK.

Contents

Introduction

I visited Yorkshire as a young bus enthusiast in 1962 when I spent several days travelling around the West and East Ridings by bus, taking many photographs. At that time, I did not realise that I was witnessing the end of an era in bus operating terms, that Yorkshire's larger company operators would be absorbed into the National Bus Company in 1969, that most municipal operators seen would be merged to form Passenger Transport Executives in 1974 and that many of the independent operators would shortly sell their businesses.

This book describes and illustrates most of the stage carriage (bus) and trolleybus operators across the traditional West and East Ridings of Yorkshire in 1962, excluding the northern tip of the West Riding beyond Skipton to Settle and Sedbergh. I was not able to get everywhere or photograph everything so I am most grateful to Michael Dryhurst, Thomas W. W. Knowles, Kevin Lane, the J. S. Cockshott Archive and the Omnibus Society for kindly allowing use of their copyright images to supplement my own pictures. Photography was very much a black and white world in 1962, therefore I wish to thank Alan Oxley, Photo Archivist of the Omnibus Society, for searching out some period colour pictures that give a glimpse of some of the varied liveries of the time. I am appreciative of advice on content received from Mike Eyre, Joe Gomall, Thomas W. W. Knowles, Geoff Lumb, Alan Oxley and members of the Omnibus Society's Provincial Historical Research Group. Omnibus Society and PSV Circle publications have been helpful in checking some details as have Ian Allan Ltd's *Buses Illustrated* magazine and the Bus Lists on the Web website.

Philip Wallis

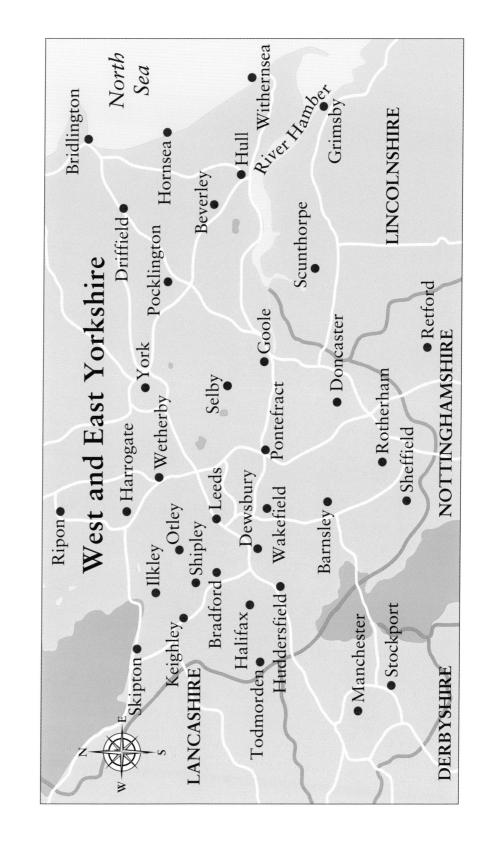

Municipal Operators

Bradford City Transport

Bradford Corporation started tramway operation in 1898 and in 1902 absorbed company-operated tramways in the city. Bradford and Leeds Corporations were joint first trolleybus operators in the country when both undertakings started services on 24 June 1911. A further trolleybus route was introduced in 1914 and growth of the system accelerated when Transport Committee policy switched to replacing many tram routes with trolleybuses from 1929 onwards. Plans to convert the last tram route in 1940 were delayed by the outbreak of the Second World War, and Bradford's final tram operated on 6 May 1950. Corporation motor buses were first operated in 1926 and their use gradually expanded, including opening services beyond the city boundary from 1928.

The title of the undertaking was changed to Bradford City Transport in March 1952. Bradford continued to back the trolleybus with a final new service to Holme Wood starting in 1960. By then the trolleybus network covered 47 route miles using 200 trolleybuses. In 1962 the Transport Committee made the fateful decision to replace the trolleybus network with motorbus operation. The first two routes to be converted were the City to Bradford Moor and Eccleshill to St Enoch's Road routes in November 1962. The conversion process lasted ten years and Bradford had the distinction of being the final UK operator of trolleybuses when its last trolleybus ran on 26 March 1972.

Bradford City Transport benefitted from the decimation of trolleybus systems elsewhere in the country, acquiring vehicles from eight other systems upon their closures in the 1950s and early 1960s. Many were rebodied for further service with handsome front-entrance East Lancashire Coachbuilders bodywork while others were broken up for spare parts. The motorbus fleet in 1962 comprised a mixture of AEC and Leyland chassis, AEC having gained dominance in supply since 1959 with Regent V chassis. A notable acquisition in 1958 had been twenty-five former London Transport RT-type AEC Regent IIIs. Joint operation took Bradford's buses to Leeds, Dewsbury and Huddersfield. The livery was light blue and cream.

Bradford City Transport was absorbed into West Yorkshire Passenger Transport Executive on 1 April 1974.

Trolleybuses new to
Bradford City Transport
seen at Saltaire in August
1962. (*Above*) 718
was a 1945 Karrier W
rebodied in 1957 with an
8-foot-wide East Lancs
body. (*Right*) 1949 BUT
9611T 743 retained
its original Roe body.
(Both Philip Wallis)

Bradford's 761 was a
1949 Weymann-bodied
BUT 9611T acquired
in 1953 from
Nottinghamshire &
Derbyshire Traction
Company. It was at
Dudley Hill in August
1962 working route
18 to Tong Cemetery.
(Philip Wallis)

Former St Helens Corporation 1951 East Lancs-bodied BUT 9611T 794 was passing through Bradford's Forster Square en route to Eccleshill. (Philip Wallis)

Bradford's bus fleet contained a good number of AEC Regent IIIs. (*Left*) 27 was a 1950 Weymann-bodied model. (*Below*) Other Regent IIIs carried East Lancs bodies with new-look bonnets over concealed radiators, as shown by 1952-model 77 emerging from Squire Lane into Duckworth Lane working circuitous route 80 from Bankfoot. (Both Philip Wallis)

Bradford acquired twenty-five former London Transport RT-type AEC Regent IIIs in 1958. Saunders-bodied 411 (former RT 170) was waiting with another RT outside the Ryco Works. (Thomas W. Knowles Collection)

Bradford's 1961 Metro-Cammell-bodied AEC Regent V 125 was at Dewsbury bus station on route 4, worked jointly with Yorkshire Woollen District. (Philip Wallis)

Doncaster Corporation Transport Department

Doncaster Corporation's first tram route opened on 2 June 1902 and its final new tram route, to Brodsworth, started on 21 February 1916. Further proposed tram routes to Armthorpe, Hatfield and Rossington were never implemented due to effects of the First World War. After the war the poor state of the tramway led the Transport Committee to recommend its abandonment. Motorbus operation had started in 1922 and such vehicles replaced trams on the Avenue Road route in 1925. The Transport Committee then decided that trolleybuses would afford more economical replacement for the remaining tram routes. The Bentley tram route was the first to be so converted on 19 August 1928 and Doncaster's last tram ran on the Brodsworth route on 8 June 1935.

The Bentley route was converted to motorbus operation on 12 February 1956 but otherwise trolleybus operation seemed secure at Doncaster. Like Bradford, Doncaster benefited from closure of trolleybus systems elsewhere and in the 1950s acquired BUT, Karrier and Sunbeam trolleybuses from four such operators. Many were rebodied for further service by Leeds-based coachbuilder Charles H. Roe, with such work continuing up to 1959. A decision was made in 1961 to convert the trolleybus system to motorbus operation. Conversion was swift, with the last trolleybus running on the Beckett Road route on 14 December 1963.

The corporation did not have a monopoly of bus services in its area. Vigorous competition in the 1920s had led to compromises leading to Doncaster operating joint services with East Midland, Rotherham Corporation, Sheffield City Transport, Yorkshire Traction and several local independents.

Doncaster's fleet in 1962 comprised seventy-three double-deck and seven single-deck motorbuses along with twenty-eight trolleybuses. AEC had dominated motorbus chassis supply to the undertaking since 1953 but Daimler CVG6 chassis were mainly chosen for trolleybus replacement in 1962. Many of these were fitted with newish Roe bodies removed from withdrawn trolleybuses and converted to half-cab configuration. Livery was maroon and white.

Doncaster Corporation Transport Department was absorbed into South Yorkshire Passenger Transport Executive on 1 April 1974.

Doncaster trolleybus 385 was a former Southend Corporation 1945 Sunbeam W rebodied by Roe in 1958. Seen along High Street in August 1962, it was withdrawn in October 1962 after which its body was converted to half-cab and transferred to new Daimler CVG6 184. (Philip Wallis)

397 originated with Mexborough & Swinton in 1943 as a single-deck Sunbeam W trolleybus. After sale to Doncaster Corporation it was rebodied by Roe in 1955. It was seen in Printing Office Street in August 1962, shortly before withdrawal the following December. (Philip Wallis)

1947 all-Leyland PD2/1 93 was temporarily withdrawn in 1963 to have a Roe body, removed from trolleybus 396, fitted. 93 then continued in service until 1973. (Philip Wallis)

Doncaster's varied fleet included 1949 Roe-bodied Daimler CVD6 113, seen along the High Street. (Philip Wallis)

1954 Roe-bodied AEC Regent III 128 was awaiting departure from Doncaster's Glasgow Paddocks on route 77 to Sheffield, operated jointly by Doncaster and Rotherham Corporations and Sheffield Transport. (Philip Wallis)

Daimler CVG6 169, fitted with a 1957 Roe body removed from trolleybus 384, had just entered service when photographed in August 1962. It was interworking with trolleybuses on the Balby route, over which trolleybuses would be completely replaced later that month. (Philip Wallis)

24 was one of a trio of 1953 Roe-bodied AEC Regal IIIs in Doncaster's fleet that had been converted to one-man operation in 1958. (Philip Wallis)

Trolleybuses were replaced on the Hexthorpe route on 19 March 1962 by one-man operated Roe-bodied AEC Reliances such as 26, photographed along the High Street in August 1962. (Philip Wallis)

Halifax Corporation Transport and Halifax Joint Omnibus Committee

Halifax Corporation started tramway operation on 9 June 1898 with three routes. The network expanded and the tramcar fleet grew to a maximum of 131 cars by 1931. The first motorbus service started on 16 October 1912. The tramway network was converted to motorbus operation in the 1930s, with the last tram route closing after 14 February 1939. Limited-scale operation of trolleybuses had taken place between 1921 and 1926. Consideration was given to replacing the trams with trolleybuses, a method of traction which might have suited the hilly nature of Halifax, but the general manager calculated that electricity costs would be too high because of the steep gradients.

The corporation faced intense competition with other bus operators in the 1920s, particularly so with Oliver and Charles Holdsworth's Hebble Bus Services. Hebble was bought by the London, Midland & Scottish and the London & North Eastern Railway companies in December 1929. This led to the setting up of the Halifax Joint Omnibus Committee (JOC) with complex revenue apportionment. Essentially money from services within the borough went to Halifax Corporation and income from those running beyond the borough went to the JOC and was then divided between the corporation and the railway companies. Corporation and JOC bus fleets were in separate ownership but shared common administration and garaging. Joint operation with Huddersfield JOC took Halifax JOC buses to Huddersfield.

Halifax's combined fleets comprised 140 double-deck and twenty-eight single-deck buses in 1962, based on a mixture of AEC, Daimler and Leyland chassis.

The railway's interest in the JOC (by then vested in British Railways) passed to the newly created National Bus Company's subsidiary Amalgamated Passenger Transport Ltd on 1 January 1969. The JOC's fleet was merged with that of nearby Todmorden JOC on 6 September 1971 to form Calderdale JOC. Calderdale JOC operated alongside Halifax Corporation until both fleets were absorbed into West Yorkshire Passenger Transport Executive on 1 April 1974.

1948 Park Royal-bodied AEC Regent III 56 in the Halifax Corporation fleet displayed the undertaking's attractive green, orange and cream livery. (The Omnibus Society)

Halifax JOC's 1954 concealed-radiator Metro-Cammell Orion-bodied Daimler CVG6 293 was photographed in the town's bus station in August 1962. (Philip Wallis)

Reversion to exposed radiators was evident in a batch of 1959 MCCW-bodied Leyland Titan PD3/4s delivered to Halifax JOC, as shown by 203 at Halifax bus station. (Philip Wallis)

The bus industry's contemporary trend towards forward entrances on double-deckers was shown by Halifax Corporation's 1960 Metro-Cammell Orion-bodied AEC Regent V 13 as it departed from the town's bus station in August 1962. (Philip Wallis)

256 was one of several 1949 Roe-bodied AEC Regal IIIs in Halifax JOC's fleet rebuilt with front entrances for one-man operation. Seen at Halifax bus station in August 1962, 256 was withdrawn the following year. (Philip Wallis)

Few Leyland Royal Tiger Worldmasters were sold in the UK, although the model sold well abroad, with around 20,000 being produced between 1954 and 1979. Halifax Corporation took ten Weymann-bodied RT3/1 models in 1958, including No. 4 seen leaving the town's bus station. (Philip Wallis)

Halifax Corporation's brand new Weymann-bodied Leyland Leopard L1 31 was photographed at the bus station in August 1962. (Philip Wallis)

Huddersfield Corporation and Huddersfield Joint Omnibus Committee

Huddersfield Corporation was the first municipal operator in the country to directly operate a tramway with the launch of steam-tram services on 11 January 1883. The system was subsequently electrified, with the first electric tram services to Outlane and Lindley starting on 14 February 1901. Eleven electric tram routes were operating by 13 July 1902.

The corporation's first motorbuses were introduced in 1920 to work shuttle services connecting with outer termini of the tramway. Other bus routes followed but experienced intensive competition from private operators. After railway companies were permitted to operate bus services in 1928, negotiations were entered into with the London, Midland & Scottish Railway, which led to the formation of the Huddersfield Joint Omnibus Committee (JOC) on 25 June 1930. Trams remained corporation-owned but buses passed into JOC ownership. A coordination agreement for bus services along the Colne valley was entered into with Hanson Buses Ltd on 23 September 1939.

Huddersfield's first trolleybus service replaced Almondbury route tramcars on 4 December 1933. This was an isolated conversion driven by the poor state of the tram track. A policy decision to convert most tram routes to trolleybus operation was made in 1936 and implemented between 1937 and 29 June 1940 when Huddersfield's last trams ran.

The Brighouse trolleybus route was cut back to Fixby (borough boundary) on 9 July 1955. Buses replaced trolleybuses on the West Vale trolleybus route on 9 November 1961. It was decided in October 1962 to convert the entire trolleybus network to bus operation. This happened progressively until Huddersfield's last trolleybuses ran on the Waterloo to Outlane route on 13 July 1968.

The combined fleets of the corporation and JOC in 1962 comprised seventy double-deck and twenty-six single-deck buses along with 116 trolleybuses. AEC chassis predominated in the bus fleet, although Leyland Titan PD3s were chosen for initial trolleybus replacement. Trolleybuses comprised Karrier, Sunbeam and BUT chassis. Fleet livery was red and cream, while trolleybuses and trolleybus-replacement Leyland Titan PD3s had painted cream fronts to enable passengers to identify them as corporation-owned vehicles as opposed to JOC, on which higher fares were charged. Joint operation took JOC buses to Bradford, Dewsbury and Halifax.

Huddersfield Corporation acquired the railway's share (latterly vested in NBC subsidiary Amalgamated Passenger Transport Ltd) in the JOC on 1 October 1969. Hanson Buses' stage carriage services were sold to the corporation on the same day. Huddersfield Corporation Passenger Transport was absorbed into West Yorkshire Passenger Transport Executive on 1 April 1974.

Above: Huddersfield Corporation 547 was a 1947 Park Royal-bodied Sunbeam MS2 trolleybus. (Michael Dryhurst)

Left: Huddersfield Corporation's newest trolleybuses comprised ten 1959 East Lancs-bodied Sunbeam S7s including 638. (Philip Wallis)

Huddersfield JOC's 1950 East Lancs-bodied AEC Regent III 158 was on stand in Lord Street during August 1962. (Philip Wallis)

The JOC's fleet included some low-bridge double-deckers such as 1955 East Lancs-bodied AEC Regent III 240, seen in Huddersfield bus station. (Philip Wallis)

Brand new Roe-bodied AEC Regent V 199 in the JOC fleet was working Golcar route 1, operated jointly with Hanson Buses. (Philip Wallis)

Left: Huddersfield Corporation's trolleybus replacement 1961 Roe-bodied Leyland Titan PD3A/2 407 displayed its cream front. (Philip Wallis)

Below: Huddersfield JOC's fleet included twenty-four single-deckers. 22 was a 1961 Roe-bodied Leyland Leopard L1. (Michael Dryhurst)

Kingston upon Hull Corporation Transport

Municipal operation of tramways in Hull started in the last years of the nineteenth century when the corporation acquired the tramways of two private companies and soon electrified the system. Hull's tramways were aligned with main roads out of the city. A new general manager, appointed in 1931, instituted a tramway replacement policy. The Victoria Pier tram route went over to motorbus operation in 1931 but most subsequent tramway replacement was by trolleybuses between 1937 and 1945.

Motorbuses had been operated briefly between 1909 and 1913. Revival of motorbus operation started in 1921 and expanded steadily. A coordination scheme was agreed with East Yorkshire Motor Services in 1934 when an inner area became exclusive corporation territory and an outer area became jointly operated. The corporation suffered badly in the Second World War, losing forty-four vehicles to enemy action in 1941.

Conversion of the trolleybus system to bus operation started on 29 January 1961 with Dairycoates route 70. Hull's last trolleybuses operated on Beverley Road route 63 on 31 October 1964.

Kingston upon Hull Corporation's fleet in 1962 comprised 155 double-deck buses, twenty single-deck buses and sixty-three double-deck trolleybuses. AEC chassis predominated in the bus fleet but purchasing policy had switched to Leyland Atlanteans in 1960. Notable acquisitions in 1961 and 1962, in order to speed up trolleybus replacement, were ten second-hand Daimlers CVG6s from Newcastle Corporation and nineteen RT-type AEC Regent IIIs from St Helens Corporation. The dwindling trolleybus fleet was based on Sunbeam chassis. Livery was blue and white, applied in a distinctive streamline style.

The coordination scheme with East Yorkshire was modified in December 1969 to cover a unified area. Bus service deregulation in October 1986 broke the coordination scheme and led to fierce competition between Kingston upon Hull City Transport (KHCT), East Yorkshire and other operators. After suffering heavy losses, KHCT was sold to Cleveland Transit in December 1993. Cleveland Transit was acquired by the Stagecoach group in November 1994, which currently brands its Hull operation as Stagecoach in Hull.

Hull Corporation's
96 was a
1948 Roe-bodied
Sunbeam F4
trolleybus.
(Michael Dryhurst)

Hull Corporation's 1955 Roe-bodied Sunbeam MF2B Coronation-class trolleybus 113 and East Yorkshire's 1962 Park Royal-bodied AEC Bridgemaster 719 met at the junction of King Edward Street with Jameson Street on 2 June 1962. (Kevin Lane Collection)

Hull Corporation's 217 was a wartime utility Guy Arab II that had been rebodied in 1949 with a Weymann body removed from a pre-war Daimler COG5. It was photographed at Ferensway coach station in July 1962 with a 'Limited Stop' display applicable to outbound journeys on certain routes between 4.30 and 6.00 p.m. on Mondays to Fridays. (Philip Wallis)

Hull's wartime Guy Arab II 239 retained its utility Massey body when seen at Ferensway coach station in July 1962. (Philip Wallis)

Hull Corporation standardised on AEC Regents for double-deck purchases between 1946 and 1953. 274, departing from Ferensway coach station, was a 1947 Weymann-bodied Regent III model. (Philip Wallis)

Six front-entrance Weymann-bodied AEC Regal IIIs joined Hull's fleet in 1949. 6 was photographed at Ferensway coach station just before a conductor could get in the way of the camera! (Philip Wallis)

Hull Corporation acquired twenty-nine second-hand double-deckers in 1961/62 to speed up trolleybus replacement. 1948 Metro-Cammell-bodied Daimler CVG6 128 came from Newcastle Corporation. (Philip Wallis)

Hull Corporation bought its first Leyland Atlanteans in 1960 and standardised on that chassis for its double-deck requirements over the next fifteen years. 360 was a 1961 Roe-bodied PDR1/1 model. (Michael Dryhurst)

Leeds City Transport

Municipal tramway operation in Leeds began in 1896 when the corporation purchased the first overhead electrically operated tramway in the country, started by the British Thompson-Houston company in 1891. Leeds' tramway grew to become one of the country's larger systems, with 433 tramcars by 1948, comprising a mixture of cars built by the undertaking and by outside builders. In 1950 ninety 'Feltham' cars were bought from London Transport. Although some routes beyond the city boundary had been replaced by motorbuses in the 1930s, the future of Leed's tramway seemed secure in the immediate post-Second World War years. A new double-deck tramcar, intended to be the first of fifty such cars, was built at Kirkstall Road works in 1948 but production models did not follow. The final extension of the tramway linked Belle Isle with Middleton in 1949. A decision was made in 1953 to replace the tramway with buses. Leeds City Transport's final three tram routes last operated on 7 November 1959.

Leeds Corporation held the joint distinction, with Bradford Corporation, of opening the country's first trolleybus routes on 24 June 1911. Two further routes were introduced in 1915 but, unlike Bradford, the trolleybus never flourished in Leeds and the last route closed in 1928.

Early small-scale motorbus operation by Leeds Corporation can be traced back to 1905. A void in operation followed until the 1920s when a small fleet was built up and increased from 1930 onwards with double-deck purchases. Leeds was technologically innovative, being an early exponent of diesel engines and pre-selective gearboxes in buses. Leeds City Transport's fleet strength was 638 buses in 1962, all bar twelve being double-deckers. Chassis makes comprised 379 AECs, 167 Leylands, seventy Daimlers, twenty Crossleys and two Guys. The great majority were bodied by Leeds coachbuilder Charles H. Roe. Livery was two shades of green. Unpainted engine covers were a distinctive feature of most exposed-radiator buses. Some routes had peak-hour 'Limited Stop' conditions, indicated by an illuminated sign on the front canopies. Joint working arrangements existed with Bradford City Transport and Yorkshire Woollen District.

Leeds City Transport was absorbed into West Yorkshire Passenger Transport Executive on 1 April 1974.

Leeds City Transport's twenty 1949 all-Crossley DD42/7s were close to the end of their service in the city when 703 was photographed at Leeds Central bus station in July 1962. (Philip Wallis)

Fleet number 355 was amongst a batch of sixty all-Leyland Titan PD2/1s delivered to Leeds in 1949/1950. It was entering Leeds Central bus station. (Philip Wallis)

Leeds City Transport's 1952 Roe-bodied AEC Regent III 658 was seen at the Central bus station in July 1962. (Philip Wallis)

The concept of Crush-Loader single-deckers, euphemistically called Standees, emerged in the mid-1950s. Leeds experimented with four such buses delivered in 1955. Roe-bodied Guy Arab UF 35 had thirty-four seats and twenty-four standing spaces. (The Omnibus Society)

Twenty Leyland Titan PD2/11s with pneumocyclic transmission entered service at Leeds in 1955. Roe-bodied 206 was in Leeds Central bus station in July 1962. (Philip Wallis)

Leeds City Transport took forty Daimler CVG6s in 1956/7. 551 carried Metro-Cammell Orion bodywork. (Philip Wallis)

1956 Roe-bodied AEC Regent V 796 displayed the unpainted bonnet favoured by Leeds City Transport on many of its double-deckers. (Philip Wallis)

Five forward-entrance Roe-bodied Daimler CVG6/LXs joined Leeds City Transport's fleet in 1962 specifically for use on Leeds–Bradford route 72, operated jointly with Bradford City Transport. This batch introduced reduced blind displays to Leeds' fleet, as shown by 574 at Hall Ings terminus in Bradford in August 1962. (Philip Wallis)

Rotherham Corporation Transport

Rotherham Corporation opened its first two electric tram routes on 31 January 1903. The network expanded over the next nine years to reach its maximum extent in 1912. The corporation's first trolleybus route opened on 5 October 1912 and the first motorbus route started on 26 July 1913. Severe competition with other operators was experienced in the 1920s and 1930s, which was partially countered by the acquisition of some competitors.

Replacement of some tram routes, mainly by trolleybuses, started on 10 June 1929 with the Broom Road route. After the last tram ran on the Canklow route on 9 July 1934, only the Templeborough route and the service to Sheffield (joint with Sheffield Corporation) remained. These were worked by eleven unusual single-ended tramcars with rear entrances, which looked more like trolleybuses. The Sheffield and Templeborough tram routes last ran on 11 December 1948 and 13 November 1949 respectively.

Rotherham's trolleybus system entered a long, slow decline when four routes or sections were converted to bus operation between 1951 and 1954. Rotherham had specified single-deck, central-entrance bodies for all its trolleybuses and motorbuses until 1946. It was considered that central entrances speeded up boarding times, allowing faster schedules requiring fewer vehicles. That policy was reconsidered in 1955 and the next year fourteen 1949/50 Daimler trolleybuses were rebodied by East Lancs with double-deck bodies. Seven single-deck Daimlers were retained to work joint services with Mexborough & Swinton until those routes were converted to bus operation on 7 March 1961. In 1962, Rotherham decided to convert its remaining trolleybus routes to bus operation with the Wickersley route going over to buses in January 1963 and the cross-town Thrybergh to Kimberworth route being the last to be operated by trolleybuses on 2 October 1965.

Rotherham Corporation Transport's fleet in 1962 was made up of ninety-eight double-deck and twenty single-deck buses, along with twenty double-deck trolleybuses. Bristol chassis had been Rotherham's preferred choice since 1925 and advance orders placed with Bristol had allowed supply of that make up to 1951, well after the sale of the Tilling group to the government in 1948 had restricted Bristol to supplying state-owned companies only. Livery was blue and cream, applied in semi-streamline style to most vehicles. Joint working agreements were in place with Doncaster Corporation, Sheffield JOC, East Midland, Mexborough & Swinton and Yorkshire Traction.

Rotherham Corporation Transport was absorbed into South Yorkshire Passenger Transport Executive on 1 April 1974.

Some of Rotherham Corporation's single-deck trolleybuses lingered at the depot after withdrawal. 1950 East Lancs-bodied Daimler CTE6 5 (FET 609) was seen heading a line of such vehicles in August 1962 before being sold for scrap the following year. (Philip Wallis)

Rotherham Corporation's 1950 Daimler CTE6 trolleybus 41 started life with a single-deck East Lancs body before being rebodied as a double-decker by Roe in 1957. It was photographed ready for a works journey from Silverwood colliery, a peak-hours branch working off the Thryberg–Kimberworth route. (The Omnibus Society)

Rotherham's post-war double-deck bus fleet was varied. (*Top*) 173 was a 1948 East Lancs-bodied Bristol K6B. (*Middle*)187 was a 1948 all-Crossley DD42/7. (*Bottom*) 229 was a 1954 Weymann-bodied Daimler CVG6. (All Philip Wallis)

Rotherham Corporation used three low-height Park Royal-bodied AEC Bridgemasters to replace its single-deck trolleybuses on the jointly operated Rotherham to Mexborough route in 1961. 139 was passing through Rawmarsh in August 1962. (Philip Wallis)

Rotherham Corporation had specified centre entrances for its single-deck buses and trolleybuses since 1927. (*Left*)1950 East Lancs-bodied Bristol L5G 115 was amongst the last such builds. (*Below*) The undertaking's modern underfloor-engine buses, such as 1959 Weymann-bodied AEC Reliance 166, came with front entrances. (Philip Wallis, The Omnibus Society)

Sheffield Transport and Sheffield Joint Omnibus Committee

Sheffield Corporation commenced tramway operation in July 1896 when it took over a company-operated horse tramway. Electrification started from 6 September 1899 and the city's basic network was established by 1905, with extensions continuing up to 1934. Fleet size had reached 468 tramcars by 1947, mostly built by the corporation. Sheffield's last new trams were thirty-five cars built by Roberts between 1950 and 1952. Ironically, before the last of the Roberts cars had been delivered, a decision was made in 1951 to convert the tramway to motorbus operation. The Fulwood to Malin Bridge was the first to go over on 6 January 1952. Sheffield's last trams ran on the Beauchief to Vulcan Road route on 8 October 1960.

Motorbus operation started in 1913 with feeder services to the tramway. Expansion followed from the 1920s. Sheffield Joint Omnibus Committee, made up of representatives from the corporation, London, Midland & Scottish and London and North Eastern Railways, was formed in 1929 to avoid wasteful competition and coordinate longer distances services. Three categories of routes and vehicle ownership were created:

'A' services were operated within the city boundary by corporation buses.

'B' services operated outside the city by vehicles jointly owned by the corporation and the railways.

'C' services were longer distance services operated by the corporation on behalf of the railways, using railway-owned buses.

Sheffield trialled Standee bus operation through a 1954 delivery of two Weymann-bodied Leyland Royal Tigers with thirty-one seats and provision for twenty-six standing passengers. The cutaway open rear entrance shown on 222 was a most unusual feature for an underfloor-engine bus. (The Omnibus Society)

Sheffield's combined fleets in 1962 comprised 798 double-deck and sixty-three single-deck buses, predominantly with AEC and Leyland chassis. Livery was cream with blue relief. Joint workings took JOC buses to Barnsley, Bradford, Buxton, Castleton, Chesterfield, Dewsbury, Doncaster, Huddersfield, Leeds, Manchester, Rotherham, Upton and Wakefield.

Sheffield Joint Omnibus Committee was wound up on 1 January 1970. The corporation took over operation of all category 'B' routes and purchased all 'B' fleet buses. Category 'C' routes were pooled with the National Bus Company (NBC) with operation passing to various NBC subsidiaries. Almost all 'C' fleet vehicles passed to Amalgamated Passenger Transport Ltd (NBC subsidiary that took over British Railways interests in the four Yorkshire Joint Committees) and were quickly dispersed amongst NBC fleets. Sheffield Transport was absorbed into South Yorkshire Passenger Transport Executive in 1 April 1974.

Sheffield's fleets were evenly split between AEC and Leyland chassis. (*Left*) 427 was an A-fleet 1950 Northern Coachbuilders AEC Regent III seen at Pond Street bus station. (*Below*) A-fleet 1951 all-Leyland Titan PD2/1 375 was photographed at Shire Green. (Both T. W. W. Knowles)

Sheffield's 862 was a 1960 Alexander-bodied AEC Regent V in the A fleet. The white-liveried buses of the Steel City seemed always to be well presented, even on drab 24 November 1962. (J. S. Cockshott Archive)

Sheffield's C-fleet buses ranged far and wide. (*Above*)1957 Eastern Coach Works-bodied Leyland Titan PD2/20 1152 was at Barnsley bus station in August 1962 working lengthy route 67 between Sheffield and Leeds (joint with Yorkshire Traction and West Riding). (*Below*)1960 Burlingham-bodied Leyland Leopard L1 1178 was passing through Ashton-under-Lyne on a return journey from Manchester to Sheffield of route 48. (Philip Wallis, Michael Dryhurst)

Sheffield received its first rear-engine double-deckers in 1959 in the form of Leyland Atlanteans. 1962 deliveries included (*Above*) Roe-bodied Leyland Atlantean 949 and (*Below*) Weymann-bodied Daimler Fleetline 953. (Both J. S. Cockshott Archive)

Opposite: Todmorden bought thirty-eight low-bridge Leyland-bodied Leyland Titan PD2s between 1947 and 1951. (*Opposite left*) 1948-model 2 was owned by the corporation. (*Opposite right*) No new buses were bought for the next ten years until 1961 when Todmorden's policy switched to the purchase of single-deck buses. The first such arrival was East Lancs-bodied Leyland Leopard L1 12, owned by British Railways. (Thomas W. W. Knowles, The Omnibus Society)

Todmorden Joint Omnibus Committee

Todmorden Corporation was the second municipal operator in the British Isles to start operating motorbuses when three routes, which superseded privately operated horse-bus services, began on 1 January 1907. Located in the heart of the Pennines at the confluence of three steep-sided valleys, the possibilities for route development were limited but in time the main services linked Todmorden with Bacup, Burnley and Summit (all in Lancashire) and Hebden Bridge.

Discussions started in 1929 between the corporation and London, Midland & Scottish Railway, which led to the establishment of the Todmorden Joint Omnibus Committee (JOC) on 1 January 1931, with both parties having equal shares. Initially vehicles were held in joint ownership but from 1947 buses were individually owned by one or other of the parties.

Todmorden Corporation and subsequently the JOC showed great loyalty to Leyland's products, with all-new vehicle purchases since 1913 having used that maker's chassis. The JOC's fleet in 1962 comprised thirty-five Leyland Titan double-deck and three Leyland Leopard single-deck buses, all bodied by Leyland bar the three single-deckers. Fleet livery was green and cream. Joint working arrangements were in force with Keighley-West Yorkshire between Hebden Bridge and Keighley and with Rochdale Corporation on a Saturday-only service between Todmorden and Rochdale.

The railway's interest in the JOC (by then vested in British Railways) passed to the newly created National Bus Company's subsidiary Amalgamated Passenger Transport Ltd on 1 January 1969. The JOC fleet was merged with that of nearby Halifax JOC on 6 September 1971 to form Calderdale JOC. Calderdale JOC was absorbed into the West Yorkshire Passenger Transport Executive on 1 April 1974.

British Electric Traction (BET) Companies

The BET group was a dominant holding company controlling bus and coach operators in England and Wales. Individual company managements had a fair degree of autonomy with running their particular businesses. No standard vehicle purchasing policy was imposed, although bodywork often had to meet BET Federation design criteria.

The BET group completed the sale of its UK bus interests to the state on 14 March 1968, with its shareholdings in subsidiary companies being taken over by the Transport Holding Company (THC), backdated to 1 March 1968. THC interests passed to the National Bus Company on 1 January 1969.

East Midland Motor Services Ltd

The bulk of East Midland's bus operations were in Derbyshire and Nottinghamshire, beyond the scope of this book. Originating as W. T. Underwood Ltd, services into Yorkshire to Doncaster were established in 1922, to Rotherham in 1923 and to Sheffield in 1925. The company's name was changed to East Midland in 1927. After brief ownership by the LMS and LNER railways, the Tilling and British Automobile Traction (TBAT) consortium acquired control on 28 February 1931. With the break-up of TBAT in 1942, control passed to the BET group.

East Midland's fleet in 1962 comprised 105 double-deck buses, ninety-five single-deck buses and thirty coaches, almost entirely with Leyland chassis. The livery was red with ivory relief. East Midland acquired Doncaster-based independent J. H. Barras (Don Motor Service) on 27 April 1962, giving it a share in the Doncaster to Rossington route, worked jointly with Doncaster Corporation and independents Blue Ensign and Rossie Motors. Within Yorkshire, other joint working agreements existed with Chesterfield Corporation, Rotherham Corporation, Sheffield JOC and Trent.

East Midland was sold to the Stagecoach group on 7 April 1989 and its operations are now an element of Stagecoach East Midlands.

East Midland's double-deck fleet comprised mainly Leyland chassis with low-bridge bodywork. 1951 all-Leyland Titan PD2/1 D 84 was at Doncaster's Glasgow Paddocks bus station in August 1962. (Philip Wallis)

1958 Weymann Orion-bodied Leyland Titan PD3/4 D 125 was setting off from Glasgow Paddocks bound for Nottingham on route 36, jointly operated with Trent route 64. (Philip Wallis)

1961 Weymann-bodied Leyland Atlantean D 151 was leaving Glasgow Paddocks working former Don Motor Services share of route 11 to New Rossington. (Philip Wallis)

East Yorkshire Motor Services Ltd

East Yorkshire was formed in August 1926 to absorb the businesses of two earlier operators. It became a BET-controlled company in 1942 with the split-up of the TBAT combine. A coordination scheme for the Hull area was entered into with Kingston upon Hull Corporation in 1934. East Yorkshire's bus services covered most of the East Riding of Yorkshire. Joint working with West Yorkshire took the company's buses to Leeds. A works service at Withernsea was operated jointly with Connor and Graham Ltd.

A distinctive characteristic of the company's double-deck buses was the Beverley Bar roof profile. The Gothic arch at Beverley, with nominal clearance of 10 feet 9 inches, would not allow even low-bridge double-deckers to pass underneath. A specially shaped roof profile was devised and fitted on almost all double-deckers to negotiate the arch.

East Yorkshire's fleet of 240 vehicles in 1962 comprised 159 double-deck buses, thirty-eight single-deck buses and forty-three coaches or dual-purpose vehicles. Chassis were predominantly Leylands but AEC became its double-deck supplier from 1956. Route numbers were used in timetables but not displayed on buses, except Bridlington town services, until the arrival of 1961 AEC Bridgemasters. Livery was primrose and blue.

East Yorkshire was acquired by the Go-Ahead group in June 2018.

1949 Roe-bodied Leyland Titan PD1A 514 was departing from Hull's Ferensway coach station in July 1962 working local route 56 to Longhill Estate, operated jointly with Hull Corporation. The characteristic Gothic roof profile of East Yorkshire's double-deckers, to pass under Beverley Bar, is evident in this view. (Philip Wallis)

Coach-specification Roe-bodied Leyland PD2/12s, such as 1952-built 568, were intended for use on East Yorkshire's longer distance services. (Philip Wallis)

1956 Willowbrook-bodied AEC Regent V 640 was passing through Driffield working lengthy route 12 from Scarborough to Hull in July 1962. (Philip Wallis)

The road surface underneath Beverley Bar was lowered in 1959 in anticipation that new low height AEC Bridgemasters would then be able to pass through the arch. After experience with four standard 1960 Bridgemasters, it was found that subsequent deliveries needed modified top-deck roof profiles to give enough clearance through the arch, as is evident on 1962 Park Royal-bodied 718 leaving Ferensway coach station in July 1962. (Philip Wallis)

East Yorkshire's Pocklington depot is reputed to have been the first major operators' depot in the country to have become fully one-man operated (OMO). 1952 Weymann-bodied Leyland Royal Tigers 595 and 599 were seen at Pocklington in July 1962 displaying triangular OMO notices in their windscreens. (Philip Wallis)

Leeds-bound 1960 OMO Leyland Tiger Cub 690 was fitted with a BET Federation-style Metro-Cammell body. It was seen at Pocklington with West Yorkshire Bristol LL5G SGW 8 behind on route 44 to Bridlington. (Philip Wallis)

Hebble Motor Services Ltd

Hebble Bus Service was formed in December 1924 by brothers Charles and Oliver Holdsworth. Hebble quickly developed a strong nucleus of services emanating from Bradford and Halifax. The LMS and LNER railways bought Hebble in December 1929, with some routes being transferred to the Halifax JOC. BET acquired a controlling interest in renamed Hebble Motor Services in 1932. The last bus service in the country to be operated by a railway company, the LMS's Halifax to Rochdale route, was taken over by Hebble on 10 December 1933.

Lengthy cross-Pennine bus routes from Burnley and Rochdale, in Lancashire, to Leeds were a feature of Hebble's operation. Joint working arrangements were in place with Bradford City Transport, Huddersfield JOC and Yorkshire Woollen District. Coaching activity was strong including excursions, coastal express services and participation in the Yorkshire–Blackpool Joint Services pool. Hebble's fleet in 1962 comprised twenty-four double-deck and thirty-one single-deck buses along with thirty-two coaches. Livery was red and cream, with a higher cream content on coaches.

Under NBC auspices, most of Hebble's bus services were absorbed by West Yorkshire RCC in 1970 or Halifax JOC in 1971. Coaching activity continued until 1 January 1974 when it was merged with Sheffield United Tours to form National Travel (North East).

Contrasting vehicle types seen in Halifax bus station working Hebble's lengthy cross-Pennine Leeds to Burnley route in August 1962.(*Above*) 267 was a 1952 Willowbrook low-bridge-bodied AEC Regent III. (*Below*) 178 was a 1956 Willowbrook-bodied AEC Reliance. (Both Philip Wallis)

Hebble's 1959 BET Federation-style Willowbrook-bodied AEC Reliance 191 was at King Street terminus in Leeds about to work cross-Pennine route 28 to Rochdale. (Philip Wallis)

Hebble's 1960 Metro-Cammell-bodied AEC Regent V 312 was in Halifax bus station working route 7 to Bradford. (Philip Wallis)

Hebble 41 was a 1955 Plaxton-bodied Commer TS3 acquired with the purchase of Ripponden & District in 1957. A windscreen sticker showed that it was bound for Blackpool. (Philip Wallis)

Mexborough & Swinton Traction Company Ltd

Mexborough & Swinton (M&S) began as a tramway operator when a service from the Rotherham borough boundary to Rawmarsh started on 1 February 1907. Joint running with Rotherham Corporation between Rotherham and Mexborough via Swinton soon followed. Trolleybus operation began on 31 August 1915 but was suspended between 1917 and 1919. The Rotherham and Mexborough tram route, M&S's last tramway service, was converted to trolleybus operation from 10 March 1929. The M&S trolleybus system was noteworthy in being operated by single-deck trolleybuses, necessitated by several low bridges. Motorbus operation had started in November 1922 with a service from Mexborough to Goldthorpe, which later passed to Yorkshire Traction. A number of other short motorbus routes were developed from 1925 onwards.

BET gained control of Mexborough & Swinton in January 1931 when it bought National Electric Construction Company, M&S's holding company.

The Ryecroft trolleybus route was replaced by single-deck buses on 27 September 1954. In 1957 M&S was amongst the first BET companies to introduce one-man operation, using high capacity Crush-Loader Leyland Tiger Cubs with, originally, provision for twenty-nine standing passengers. The Conisbrough to Manvers Main route was converted to bus operation on 1 January 1961 and the last trolleybus route, Rotherham to Conisbrough, followed on 27 March 1961. This marked the end of electrically powered traction by a BET company. The replacement low-bridge Leyland Atlanteans were the first double-deck buses to have been operated by M&S.

Mexborough & Swinton's fleet in 1962 comprised twelve double-deck and nineteen single-deck buses along with three coaches, all Leylands apart from one Ford coach. Livery was green and cream. Joint operation continued with Rotherham Corporation on certain routes.

Mexborough & Swinton was absorbed by Yorkshire Traction on 1 October 1969.

Mexborough & Swinton 15 was one of two pre-war Northern Counties-bodied Leyland Titan TD5s acquired from Southdown in 1961 and photographed in Rawmarsh depot yard in August 1962. (Philip Wallis)

1957 standee Weymann-bodied Leyland Tiger Cub 52 had a good passenger load as it passed through Rawmarsh in August 1962. (Philip Wallis)

Weymann low-bridge-bodied Leyland Atlantean 5 was one of eleven such buses that replaced Mexborough & Swinton's trolleybuses in March 1961. (Philip Wallis)

Yorkshire Traction Company Ltd

The origin of Yorkshire Traction was with BET subsidiary Barnsley & District, formed in 1902 to operate an electric tramway. Motorbus operation started in 1913 and expanded rapidly, particularly in the 1920s and, to reflect its wider area of operation, the company's name was changed to Yorkshire Traction in January 1929. Its single-route tramway through Barnsley was converted to motorbus operation in 1930 and Yorkshire Traction buses replaced the Dearne District tramway in 1933. Multiple acquisitions of competitive operators in the 1930s consolidated Yorkshire Traction's position as the premier operator in a densely populated area lying between Huddersfield and Doncaster.

Yorkshire Traction's fleet in 1962 was made up of 148 double-deck buses, 178 single-deck buses and forty-four coaches. Leyland chassis predominated in the fleet, a position that manufacturer had enjoyed since Tracky's earliest days. Joint services were operated with Doncaster Corporation, North Western, Rotherham Corporation, Sheffield JOC, South Yorkshire Motors, West Riding and Yorkshire Woollen District. Yorkshire Traction was a participant in the Yorkshire Services and Yorkshire–Blackpool Joint Services express service pools. Livery was red and ivory.

Yorkshire Traction was acquired by the Stagecoach group in December 2005 and its operations are now an element of Stagecoach Yorkshire.

1948 all-Leyland Titan PD2/1 775 was amongst Yorkshire Traction's oldest buses when photographed at Barnsley bus station in August 1962. (Philip Wallis)

Yorkshire Traction was an early operator of rear-engine Leyland Atlanteans as exemplified by (*Above*) 1959 Weymann low-bridge-bodied PDR1/1 model 1153 but did not buy any more until 1964. In the interim Tracky reverted to traditional front-engine double-deckers such as (*Below*) 1962 Northern Counties-bodied Leyland Titan PD3A/1 1223, seen at Barnsley bus station. (Both Philip Wallis)

Yorkshire Traction had a long history of rebuilding older chassis to create new buses. 1191 used an earlier Leyland PS2 chassis, which was fitted with a new Roe high-bridge body before the re-registered bus entered service in 1961. (The Omnibus Society)

1957 Willowbrook-
bodied Leyland Tiger
Cub 1098 was in
Barnsley bus station
in August 1962.
(Philip Wallis)

1962 36-foot
Willowbrook-bodied
Leyland Leopard
1237 was loading in
Barnsley bus station
for heavily used route
23 to Thurnscoe.
(Philip Wallis)

Yorkshire Traction had a varied coach fleet. (*Above*) Ex-Camplejohn Brothers 1950 Yeates-bodied Lancet 135 was in the sole Dennis remaining in Tracky's fleet when photographed at Manchester's Lower Mosley Street in August 1962. (*Below*) 1961 Burlingham-bodied Leyland Tiger Cub 1209 had arrived at London's Victoria coach station at the end of a Yorkshire Services Pool journey. (Philip Wallis, Michael Dryhurst)

Yorkshire Woollen District Transport Company Ltd

BET-controlled Yorkshire (Woollen District) Electric Tramways commenced operating tramways in the Heavy Woollen District of the West Riding in 1903. Expansion was such that by 1926 it was operating sixty-nine tramcars. Motorbus operation had been inaugurated in 1913 and by 1926 the company was operating fifty-one buses.

The company was a participant in the Tyne–Tees–Mersey Limited Stop Services pool from its establishment on 15 May 1929 and became a member of the Yorkshire–Blackpool Joint Services pool when established in December 1934.

Tramway services were converted to motorbus operation from 1932 and the last tram ran on 31 October 1934. The tramway company was wound up and assets transferred to newly formed Yorkshire Woollen District Transport Co. Ltd. Its core area of operation continued to be focussed on the Heavy Woollen District around Batley, Dewsbury, Heckmondwike and Ossett, with other services taking the company's buses to many other West Riding cities and towns. Manchester was reached by hourly route X12, joint with North Western RCC. Other routes were operated jointly with Bradford City Transport, Hebble, Huddersfield JOC, Leeds City Transport, Sheffield JOC, West Riding and Yorkshire Traction.

Yorkshire Woollen District's fleet in 1962 contained 147 double-deck buses, seventy-three single-deck buses and fifty-six coaches. Leyland chassis predominated numerically but all vehicle purchases since 1958 had been AECs. An unrelieved red livery was applied to all double-deck and some single-deck buses. Other single-deck buses and all coaches were painted cream with red relief.

Yorkshire Woollen District has been part of the Arriva group since 1997 and its operations now form an element of Arriva Yorkshire.

508 originated with Maidstone & District as a 1943 Weymann-bodied utility Guy Arab II. After sale to Yorkshire Woollen it was fitted with a new Roe high-bridge body as seen when photographed at Dewsbury bus station in August 1962. (Philip Wallis)

Yorkshire Woollen's 630 was a 1948 Leyland Tiger PS1, which originally carried a Brush single-deck body. It was rebodied with a Metro-Cammell Orion double-deck body in 1955 and was leaving Dewsbury bus station on route 4 to Bradford, operated jointly with Bradford City Transport. (Philip Wallis)

Dewsbury local services were identified by route letters, rather than numbers. Metro-Cammell Orion-bodied AEC Regent V 836 was passing through Dewsbury bus station working Ravensthorpe to Ossett route B. (Philip Wallis)

After several years of buying AEC Regent Vs for its new double-deck needs, Yorkshire Woollen took Leyland Titan PD3A/1s in 1962 including 894, seen departing from Halifax bus station bound for Leeds on route 24. (Philip Wallis)

1950 Willowbrook-bodied Leyland Tiger PS2/5 724 was at Lower Mosley Street in Manchester about to depart on a route X12 journey across the Pennines to Bradford in July 1962. (Michael Dryhurst)

Only ninety Leyland-MCW Olympic integrals were sold in the UK, although the model did well in export markets such as Cuba and South Africa. Yorkshire Woollen received ten including 1951 HR44 model 735. (Philip Wallis)

Newly delivered BET Federation-style Marshall-bodied AEC Reliance 878 had paused at Halifax bus station in August 1962 on two-hour journey time route 2 between Ossett and Keighley. (Philip Wallis)

Jointly owned Company

County Motors (Lepton) Ltd

County Motors began operation on 11 October 1919 with a route from Huddersfield to Flockton. Further motorbus routes to Wakefield and Dewsbury were introduced in 1923. The company was sold in August 1927 to a consortium of Barnsley & District (forerunner of Yorkshire Traction), West Riding and Yorkshire Woollen District.

County Motors' vehicle purchasing policy mirrored that of Yorkshire Traction for single-deck buses and West Riding for double-deckers – extending to the purchase of two Guy Wulfrunians in 1961. County's services were included in Yorkshire Woollen District's timetable books.

County Motors' fleet in 1962 comprised seventeen double-deck and four single-deck buses along with two coaches. The livery was blue and cream.

After all three holding companies became state-owned THC subsidiaries management control of County Motors passed to Yorkshire Traction in 1968 prior to full absorption on 1 January 1969.

County's 1958 Roe low-bridge-bodied Guy Arab IV 93 was photographed in Lord Street, Huddersfield. (The Omnibus Society)

County Motors' two 1961 Roe-bodied Guy Wulfrunians had but a short life with the company before being moved to West Riding in 1963. 100 was photographed in August 1962 with a Wolverhampton trade plate in its windscreen suggesting it was going back to Guy Motors for attention. This bus was later scrapped but a kinder fate awaited sister vehicle 99, which has been preserved. (The Omnibus Society)

1959 Willowbrook-bodied Leyland Tiger Cub 95 was seen in Lord Street, Huddersfield. (Michael Dryhurst)

British Transport Commission (BTC) Company

The state-owned British Transport Commission controlled many bus and coach operators in England, Wales and Scotland. It also had minority shareholdings in some BET companies, gained through nationalisation of the main line railway companies in 1948. The Tilling Association Ltd coordinated administration and central purchasing for English and Welsh operators within the group for which vehicle purchasing policy was almost entirely restricted to state-owned Bristol chassis and Eastern Coach Works bodywork.

The BTC was abolished under the Transport Act 1962 and its provincial road passenger transport interests in England and Wales were vested in the Transport Holding Company (THC) from 1 January 1963. The THC absorbed BET's UK bus interests from 1 March 1968 and English and Welsh operators were incorporated into the National Bus Company on 1 January 1969.

West Yorkshire Road Car Company Ltd

The origin of West Yorkshire was with the Harrogate Road Car Company, formed in December 1906. A controlling interest was acquired by the TBAT grouping in 1924. The company's name was changed to West Yorkshire Road Car Company on 5 December 1927. Rapid expansion was achieved between 1926 and 1936, both by route development and acquisition of many independent operators. West Yorkshire became controlled by the Tilling group in 1942 when TBAT's interests were split between BET and Tilling.

An interesting aspect of the company's activities was the operation of former municipal services in Keighley and York. Keighley-West Yorkshire Services had been formed on 1 October 1932 to operate local services on a shared basis with Keighley Corporation. The York-West Yorkshire Joint Committee was formed on 1 April 1934 with an operating agreement similar to that at Keighley. West Yorkshire provided the vehicles in both instances.

West Yorkshire's core operating area was north from Bradford and Leeds to Skipton, Harrogate and York. Joint bus routes were run with East Yorkshire, Samuel Ledgard and United Automobile. Keighley-West Yorkshire operated joint services with Burnley, Colne and Nelson JTC and Todmorden JOC. West Yorkshire was a participant in three express service pools: Tyne-Tees-Mersey Limited Stop Services, Yorkshire-Blackpool Joint Services and Yorkshire Services. Fleet strength in 1962 (including Keighley-West Yorkshire and York-West Yorkshire) comprised 286 double-deck buses, 178 single-deck buses and sixty-one coaches – all with Bristol chassis bar one Bedford OB used on the City of York Tour. Livery was red and white.

West Yorkshire was incorporated into the Transdev group in January 2006.

Right: KDG 21 comprised a 1938 Bristol K5G chassis fitted with a new Eastern Coach Works body in 1949. It displayed a Keighley-West Yorkshire fleet name when working Keighley local service 6 in May 1962. (J. S. Cockshott Archive)

All West Yorkshire Bristol K-derivative chassis carried low-bridge bodies except those of York-West Yorkshire, which had high-bridge bodies. (*Previous page bottom*) York-West Yorkshire YDG 87 was rebuilt from a 1939 Bristol K5G chassis in 1955 and fitted with a new Eastern Coach Works high-bridge body. (*Above*) The standard fifty-five-seat Eastern Coach Works low-bridge body, as fitted to 1953 Bristol KSW6G DGW 5, is shown in this July 1962 shot at Vicar Lane bus station in Leeds. (*Below*) Eastern Coach Works-bodied Bristol Lodekkas succeeded K-derivatives as the standard double-deck bus with BTC operators, illustrated by West Yorkshire's 1962 FS6B model DX 127. (All Philip Wallis)

Some York-West Yorkshire single-deckers had indicator boxes flush with the roof in order to pass under a particularly low railway bridge near Leeman Road terminus of route 7. 1948 Eastern Coach Works-bodied Bristol L5G YSG 129 was one such. (Philip Wallis)

Eastern Coach Works-bodied Bristol LS types formed BTC operators' standard single-deck intake for much of the 1950s. West Yorkshire's 1955 LS5G SUG 44 was to dual-purpose specification, its extra seating comfort being well suited to three-hour journey route 46 between Leeds and Hull. (Philip Wallis)

The only non-Bristol chassis in West Yorkshire's 1962 fleet was 1947 Duple Vista-bodied Bedford OB CP 1 used on the City of York Tour. (Philip Wallis)

It was common practice for operators to hire coaches that had worked north on Forces Leave express services for peak weekend duties. Wilts & Dorset's Eastern Coach Works-bodied Bristol LS6G 546 would have set off from military establishments on Salisbury Plain on a Friday afternoon to reach Leeds. It was then hired by West Yorkshire over the weekend before returning south on the Sunday evening. (J. S. Cockshott Archive)

Other Large Operators

Certain group operators with main operations substantially outside Yorkshire worked bus services into the West and East Ridings, some jointly operated. These included Lincolnshire Road Car Company Ltd (BTC) with routes into Bawtry, Doncaster and Goole; North Western Road Car Company Ltd (BET), which reached Barnsley, Bradford, Halifax, Huddersfield and Sheffield; and Trent Motor Traction Company Ltd (BET), which reached Doncaster from Nottingham. Ribble Motor Services Ltd (BET) had a depot in Skipton from which it worked local services and others into Lancashire. United Automobile Services Ltd (BTC), with a significant presence in the North Riding of Yorkshire, reached Bridlington, Harrogate, Leeds and York.

Lancashire municipal Burnley, Colne & Nelson Joint Transport Committee's buses operated to Keighley, jointly with West Yorkshire, and Skipton, jointly with Ribble, as well as to certain other towns and villages, such as Barnoldswick, then in Yorkshire. Derbyshire municipal operator Chesterfield Corporation Transport Department operated between Chesterfield and Sheffield on route 12 jointly with Sheffield JOC and on routes 62 and 64 jointly with East Midland and Sheffield JOC.

Above and over leaf above: Lincolnshire RCC worked into Doncaster from Scunthorpe and Gainsborough. 1959 Eastern Coach Works-bodied Bristol LD5G 2370 was seen at Glasgow Paddocks in February 1962 and Bristol MW5G 2677 was on layover there having worked a route 105 journey from Gainsborough. (Both J. S. Cockshott Archive)

North Western's 1953 Weymann-bodied Leyland Royal Tiger 535 was seen in Bradford's Chester Street bus station with a full passenger load for its route X12 journey to Manchester, operated jointly with Yorkshire Woollen. (J. S. Cockshott Archive)

Ribble had allocated brand new Weymann-bodied coach specification Leyland Atlantean PDR1/1 1283 to hourly Skipton to Manchester route X43 when photographed at Skipton bus station on 27 May 1962. (J. S. Cockshott Archive)

Trent's 1960 Roe-bodied Leyland Atlantean PDR1/1 1078 was at Doncaster's Glasgow Paddocks terminus of Nottingham route 64, operated jointly with East Midland route 36. (J. S. Cockshott Archive)

United Automobile's 1958 Eastern Coach Works-bodied Bristol LD6B BL 23 was seen at the Harrogate bus station terminus of route 126 to Ripon, operated jointly with West Yorkshire route 36. (J. S. Cockshott Archive)

Burnley, Colne & Nelson JTC's 1953 East Lancs-bodied Leyland Titan PD2/12 215 was seen at Keighley bus station. (J. S. Cockshott Archive)

Chesterfield Corporation's Metro-Cammell-bodied Daimler Fleetline 302 was departing from Sheffield's Pond Street bus station on route 12 to Chesterfield, jointly operated with Sheffield Transport. (J. S. Cockshott Archive)

Larger Independents

T. Burrows & Sons Ltd

Burrows of Wombwell was a long-established operator particularly noted for its lengthy 43-mile bus route between Rawmarsh and Leeds, worked by a mixture of elderly and more modern buses. Burrows 1962 fleet comprised nine double-deck buses and twenty single-deck buses and coaches. The livery was red with cream relief.

Founder Tom Burrows died in 1965.The bus route was jointly acquired by West Riding and Yorkshire Traction on 22 October 1966. Burrows' extensive coaching and contract activities continued until 1973.

(*Above*) GYE 76 was a former London Transport wartime utility Daimler CWA6. It was rebodied with a high-bridge Burlingham body in 1957 and was photographed at Leeds Central bus station. (*Below*) 1956 Roe-bodied AEC Regent V PWY 943 was new to Burrows and was seen at Barnsley bus station in August 1962. (Both Philip Wallis)

Hanson Buses Ltd

The Hanson family developed successful road haulage, bus and coach operations from nineteenth-century origins in cartage. Joseph Hanson & Sons started running bus services from Huddersfield in the 1920s and Hanson Buses Ltd was registered on 25 April 1935. A coordination agreement for services along the Colne valley was entered into with Huddersfield JOC on 23 September 1939, in mileage proportions of 42 per cent Hanson and 58 per cent JOC.

Hanson Buses' association with Yorkshire's AEC distributor Tillotson allowed it to secure new chassis frames, which were assembled with refurbished units, fitted with new Roe bodies and registered as new AEC Hansons in the 1950s and 1960s. Hanson's fleet in 1962 comprised seven double-deck and sixteen single-deck buses along with twenty-five coaches, made up of thirty-three AEC or AEC Hanson, nine Ford and six Bedford chassis. The livery was dark red.

Hanson Buses Ltd was sold to Huddersfield Corporation on 1 October 1969. Hanson's coaching business continued until 1 May 1974 when it was sold to West Yorkshire PTE.

Hanson's 1948 Duple-bodied Albion Valkyrie 249 became a tuition vehicle with the Hanson School of Motoring in 1962. It was seen earlier when in use as a bus. (The Omnibus Society)

Hanson Buses' 1951 Roe-bodied AEC Regal IV 304 was passing Huddersfield Corporation's 1954 East Lancs-bodied AEC Regent III 232 in the town centre. (Michael Dryhurst)

1961 Roe-bodied AEC Hanson Regent III 361 was loading in Huddersfield bus station for a journey over the Pennines to Oldham in Lancashire. (J. S. Cockshott Archive)

Hanson's 1961 Plaxton-bodied Ford Thames Trader coach 367 was passing through Huddersfield in August 1962 with a full passenger load. (Philip Wallis)

Executors of Samuel Ledgard Ltd

Publican Samuel Ledgard of Armley entered the haulage business in 1906. In 1912 he purchased his first petrol-engine chassis with a demountable charabanc body and in 1913 operated weekly services to Blackpool and Scarborough. The coach business was developed after the First World War and Ledgard's first bus service, between Leeds and Otley, started in 1924. The bus network developed mainly through acquisitions of other operators, the most significant being B&B Tours in 1935, which gave Ledgard a concentration of services in the area between Bradford, Ilkley and Leeds. This was shared territory with West Yorkshire RCC and an uneasy alliance was formed between the two operators with some joint operation. Over the years, West Yorkshire made several approaches seeking to acquire Ledgard's business.

After Samuel Ledgard's death in 1952, his executors ran the business, renaming subsidiary company Cream Bus to Samuel Ledgard (Ilkley) Ltd and B&B Tours to Samuel Ledgard (Bradford) Ltd.

Ledgard's fleet was a delight to the enthusiast because of its variety. Samuel Ledgard himself had mostly bought new buses and coaches but his executor's policy moved mainly to second-hand purchase. The fleet in 1962 was made up of sixty-three double-deck buses, six single-deck buses and eighteen coaches. Chassis makes comprised AEC, Albion, Atkinson, Bedford, Bristol, Daimler, Foden, Guy, Leyland and Maudslay. Livery was blue and white.

The Ledgard businesses were sold to West Yorkshire RCC on 15 October 1967. Operation of three routes passed to Leeds City Transport with the Leeds–Pudsey–Bradford route becoming jointly operated with Bradford City Transport.

Ledgard's Executors did occasionally buy new vehicles. 1953 U was one of six Roe-bodied AEC Regent Vs to join the fleet in 1957. (Philip Wallis)

GHN 840 was one of five former United Automobile Eastern Coach Works-bodied Bristol K6As acquired in 1959 to replace single-deckers on the Otley to Horsforth route. (The Omnibus Society)

Four former Exeter Corporation 1948 Brush-bodied Daimler CVD6s were bought by Ledgard in 1960 including JFJ 55, seen in Otley. (Philip Wallis)

SDU 711 started life in 1956 as a Willowbrook-bodied Daimler CVG6 demonstrator, which was exhibited at the 1956 and 1958 Commercial Motor Shows. It joined Ledgard's fleet in 1960. (Philip Wallis)

BCK 414 was one of four ex-Ribble 1947 all-Leyland Titan PD1As acquired by Ledgard in 1961. It was photographed in King Street, Leeds, during July 1962. (Philip Wallis)

Ledgard's 1962 acquisitions included five 1948 East Lancs-bodied AEC Regent IIIs formerly with Rochdale Corporation. GDK 402 was departing from Vicar Lane bus station in Leeds in July 1962 on the Rawdon service, operated jointly with West Yorkshire. (Philip Wallis)

1949 Plaxton-bodied Foden PVSC6 coach MUA 864 was seen outside Ledgard's Otley depot in August 1962. (Philip Wallis)

NWW 806 was one of a pair of 1954 Burlingham-bodied Atkinson Alphas acquired by Ledgard with its takeover of J. W. Kitchin's business in 1957. It was loading in Otley bus station during August 1962. (Philip Wallis)

South Yorkshire Motors Ltd

South Yorkshire was an old established operator based at Pontefract, which maintained regular frequency trunk routes between Leeds and Doncaster, Pontefract and Barnsley (joint with Yorkshire Traction), Doncaster and Selby and a local service to Ferrybridge. Its 1962 fleet comprised eighteen double-deck and two single-deck buses, presented in a light blue, dark blue and cream livery. South Yorkshire was also a Ford Motor Company main dealer.

South Yorkshire Motors was sold to Caldaire Holdings on 8 July 1994. Caldaire also controlled West Riding by that date.

Above: South Yorkshire's 1951 all-Leyland Titan PD2/12 74 was photographed at Barnsley bus station working the Pontefract route. (Philip Wallis)

Left: 1957 Park Royal-bodied Leyland Titan PD2/20 79 was on stand at Leeds Central bus station. (Philip Wallis)

81 had originated as a 1950 Burlingham-bodied Albion Valiant CX 37 single-deck coach. The chassis was rebodied with a new Roe low-bridge body in 1958 and re-registered TWY 8. It was seen departing from Leeds Central bus station bound for Doncaster. (The Omnibus Society)

West Riding Automobile Company Ltd

West Riding was an independent operator in the sense that it was not part of the BET or BTC groupings but it was a publicly quoted company with its shares traded on the London Stock Exchange.

West Riding began as a tramway operator when it acquired the Wakefield & District Light Railway company in 1905. Motorbus operation was started in 1922 and tram services were converted to motorbus operation between 1925 and 1932. West Riding took over substantial 150 vehicle independent operator J. Bullock & Sons in 1950. This merger gave the enlarged company a strong foothold across a wide area bounded by Leeds and York in the north and Doncaster in the south.

West Riding was the only volume purchaser of the ill-fated Guy Wulfrunian double-decker, developed in the late 1950s by Guy Motors in close collaboration with the company. The Wulfrunian was designed with future one-man operation in mind and had a front entrance, front-mounted engine and a staircase on the nearside immediately after the entrance. Other revolutionary features for its day were air suspension and disc brakes. Starting in 1959, West Riding ultimately took 126 of the 137 Wulfrunians built and acquired four more second hand. Lack of Wulfrunian sales success elsewhere was a major factor in pushing Guy Motors into receivership in 1961.

West Riding's fleet in 1962 comprised 335 double-deck and seventy-one single-deck buses along with thirty coaches. 166 vehicles were based on Leyland chassis, fifty-six on Guy, 102 on AEC, nine on Daimler and three on Seddon chassis. Leeds-built Roe bodywork was fitted to 315 vehicles. Fleet livery was green and cream but, due to differing fare structures, buses used on former tramway routes were painted red and cream. Joint operating agreements existed with Sheffield JOC, Yorkshire Woollen District and Yorkshire Traction.

West Riding was sold to the Transport Holding Company on 30 October 1967 and became a constituent of the National Bus Company on 1 January 1969.

West Riding was
still running some
wartime utility Roe
low-bridge-bodied Guy
Arab IIs in 1962 such as
593 seen entering Leeds
Central bus station
in July of that year.
(Philip Wallis)

1948 all-Leyland
Titan PD2/1 661 was
photographed in Selby
Market Place with the
town's historic abbey
in the background.
(Thomas W. W. Knowles)

West Riding buses used
on tram replacement
services featured
centre entrances and
were painted red.
When the new Guy
Wulfrunians arrived,
some superseded buses
were repainted green for
use on other services.
1949 Roe-bodied AEC
Regent III 115 was
seen in Wakefield bus
station in August 1962.
(Philip Wallis)

West Riding 325 was a 1949 Roe-bodied Daimler CVD6 acquired with J. Bullock & Sons' business in 1950. It was photographed in 1962 at Doncaster's Marshgate bus station. (Thomas W. W. Knowles)

West Riding built up a sizeable fleet of Roe low-bridge-bodied Guy Arab IVs. 1957-built 819 was entering Leeds Central bus station in July 1962. (Philip Wallis)

1961 red- and cream-liveried Guy Wulfrunian (*Above*) 876 was photographed at Cross York Street bus station in Leeds, terminus for West Riding's tram replacement bus routes. (*Below*) Green- and cream-liveried Wulfrunian 905 was on layover at Leeds Central bus station before working a route 163 journey to Castleford in July 1962. The lower steps of the nearside staircase may be seen inside its entrance. (Both Philip Wallis)

West Riding's 1948 Roe-bodied AEC Regal III 652 was seen at Castleford. (The Omnibus Society)

West Riding's final batch of front-engine single-deckers comprised twelve 1952 Roe-bodied Leyland Tiger PS2/12s including 736, seen entering Leeds Central bus station. (Philip Wallis)

York Pullman Bus Company Ltd

York Pullman had been formed in 1926. It held licences for eight stage carriage services from York, as well two licences for excursions and tours from York. Its 1962 fleet comprised five single-deck and seven double-deck buses along with ten coaches, all based at a spacious garage in Navigation Road, York. Livery was maroon, yellow and ivory.

 The York Pullman trading name, along with twenty coaches, was sold to Hull City Transport in February 1990. The remaining operation traded as Reynard Buses Ltd for a few months until acquired by Yorkshire Rider on 24 July 1990. The York Pullman trading name was revived in April 2007 by Tom James of K & J Travel, York. That business continues to trade successfully as The York Pullman Bus Company.

Left: Several York Pullman single-deckers were fitted with Hull-built Barnaby bodywork including 1953 AEC Regal III 62, seen in York in August 1962. (Philip Wallis)

Below: York Pullman's 1955 Roe-bodied AEC Regent III 67 was photographed at the Helperby terminus of a route to York. The coach garage in the background belonged to E & G Brown of Helperby. (J. S. Cockshott Archive)

Some Other Independents

Barnsley and Huddersfield Areas

Right: Baddeley Brothers Ltd was founded in 1925 at Holmfirth and operated three bus routes in addition to coaching activities. 1953 all-Sentinel STC6 OUP 578 was originally a Sentinel demonstrator subsequently operated by Trimdon Motor Services before passing to Baddeley Brothers in 1960. Baddeley Brothers was sold to West Yorkshire PTE on 24 March 1976. (The Omnibus Society)

Ideal Service was the fleet name used by Robert Taylor & Sons and by H. Wray & Sons serving a common route between Barnsley and Pontefract using completely separate fleets. (*Previous page bottom*) Taylor's YWT 972 had originated as a 1947 single-deck Leyland Tiger PS1 coach which had been rebuilt and rebodied with a low-bridge double-deck Roe body in 1959. It was seen at Pontefract bus station. (*Above*) Wray's ex-Ribble 1947 Brush-bodied Leyland Titan PD1 BCK 458 was at Barnsley bus station. Taylor's share of Ideal Service was acquired by Yorkshire Traction on 1 April 1967 and Wray's share passed to Yorkshire Traction on 1 April 1974. (Thomas W. W. Knowles, Philip Wallis)

J. W. Mosley & Sons operated a bus route between Barnsley and Higham. Unusual Mulliner-bodied Guy Warrior UWW 769, photographed in Barnsley bus station, was new in 1957 to Doncaster independent Blue Line and passed to Mosley in 1961. Mosley's bus route was taken over by Yorkshire Traction on 1 May 1965 but coaching activities continued. (Thomas W. W. Knowles)

Larratt Pepper & Sons Ltd operated a daily service between Barnsley and Thurnscoe. (*Above*) 1955 Willowbrook coach-bodied AEC Reliance PWR 403 was loading at Barnsley bus station. (*Below*) Pepper hired 1961 Duple Midland-bodied Ford Thames Trader 1456 PT from dealer Hughes of Bradford for several months in 1962. Double-width doors for one-man operation were specified by original operator Trimdon Motor Services. Pepper's bus route was acquired by Yorkshire Traction on 13 May 1978 but coaching activities continued. (Both Philip Wallis)

Arthur Rowe & Sons (Cudworth) Ltd operated a daily service between Barnsley and Royston. Ex-Ribble 1951 'White Lady' East Lancs-bodied Leyland Titan PD2/3 DCK 216 was loading in Barnsley bus station in August 1962. Rowe's bus route was taken over by Yorkshire Traction on 1 October 1969 but coaching activities continued. (Philip Wallis)

Dewsbury Area

J. J. Longstaff & Sons Ltd and Joseph Wood & Son operated daily services between Dewsbury and Mirfield over identical routeing that was also covered by Yorkshire Woollen District route 11. The three operators coordinated timetables to give a twenty-minute headway but there was no formal joint working agreement. (*Opposite below*) Longstaff's 1949 Cravens-bodied AEC Regent III KGK 759, former London Transport RT 1500, was photographed at Mirfield. (*Above*) Wood operated former Baxter of Airdrie 1949 Crossley DD42/7 EVD 406, which had been rebodied by Roe in 1954. This bus has been preserved. Longstaff's business was sold to local coach operator A. Lyles & Sons of Batley on 31 December 2011. Joseph Wood & Son was sold to Gobig Ltd (associated with Abbeyways of Halifax) in July 1983. (J. S. Cockshott Archive, Thomas W. W. Knowles)

Doncaster Area

Doncaster had long been stronghold of independent bus operation. Industrialisation of the town and its surrounding semi-rural areas increased in the 1920s and collieries opened up in villages east and south of the town. This period saw the emergence of local bus proprietors who engaged in fierce completion for custom, both amongst themselves and with established operators, with over thirty proprietors working into the borough by 1928. The 1930 Road Traffic Act's licensing system stabilised operations. By 1962 fourteen independents still served Doncaster (net of J. H. Barras' sale to East Midland on 27 April 1962). Several Doncaster independents' fleets included large capacity double-deckers bought new, an indication of the profitability of some routes. Some services were operated jointly between independents and Doncaster Corporation.

Retirement of proprietors led to the sale of many Doncaster independents to South Yorkshire PTE.

Blue Ensign's (G. H. Ennifer Ltd) 1948 Scottish Commercial-bodied Crossley DD42/7 was seen at Doncaster's Glasgow Paddocks working the Church Lane route with Doncaster Corporation's 1950 Roe-bodied Daimler CVD6 117 standing behind on the Rossington route, jointly operated by the corporation, Blue Ensign and East Midland. The company was renamed Blue Ensign Coaches Ltd in May 1971 and sold to South Yorkshire PTE on 1 April 1978. (The Omnibus Society)

Blue Line (Samuel Morgan Ltd) and Reliance (R. Store Ltd) had been in common ownership since 1949. The companies ran several bus routes out of Doncaster, either jointly operated between the two companies or with other operators. Both concerns favoured Guy chassis as shown by (*Above*) Blue Line's 1956 Burlingham-bodied Guy Arab IV SWU 876 at Doncaster's Christ Church terminus and (*Opposite above*) Reliance's 1957 Burlingham-bodied Guy Arab IV TYG 4 approaching Christ Church in August 1962. Both businesses were sold to South Yorkshire PTE on 29 March 1979. Vehicles remained licensed to the companies until August 1980. (The Omnibus Society, Philip Wallis)

Felix Motors Ltd ran on jointly operated services to Armthorpe and to Moorends. Smartly presented in plum, crimson and cream livery, 1956 Roe-bodied AEC Regent V 35 was photographed at Christ Church, Doncaster, in August 1962. Felix Motors was sold to South Yorkshire PTE on 1 April 1976. (Philip Wallis)

T. W. Holling from Askern operated a Saturday-only route into Doncaster. 1961 Willowbrook-bodied Leyland Leopard L2 WJU 406 joined the fleet in 1962 after being a demonstration vehicle for its bodybuilder. Holling's Doncaster route ceased in 1967. (Thomas W. W. Knowles Collection)

Leon Motor Services Ltd operated between Doncaster, Finningley and Misson. Leon ran several Daimler double-deckers including 1961 Roe-bodied Daimler CD650/30 57 departing from Glasgow Paddocks. Its chassis had been exhibited by Daimler at the 1958 Commercial Motor Show. Leon Motor Services, Doncaster's last surviving traditional independent, was sold to ITG-MASS Transit, North Anston, on 1 February 2004. (Philip Wallis)

Premier (Harold Wilson Ltd) operated between Doncaster and Moorends jointly with Felix Motors and T. Severn. Premier's 1959 Roe-bodied Guy Arab IV SWT 644, sporting deep-blue and primrose livery, was photographed at Christ Church terminus. Premier was sold to South Yorkshire PTE on 27 June 1988. (Philip Wallis)

Rossie Motors (Rossington) Ltd operated on two routes into Doncaster jointly with Blue Ensign, Doncaster Corporation and East Midland. Rossie's former Doncaster Corporation 1949 Roe-bodied Daimler CVD6 GDT 421 (right) had arrived at Glasgow Paddocks followed by Lincolnshire RCC's 1959 ECW-bodied Bristol MW5G 2235 on Express Service 126 from Scunthorpe. Rossie Motors was sold to South Yorkshire PTE on 21 May 1980. (The Omnibus Society)

T. Severn & Sons Ltd double-deck fleet in 1962 was based entirely on Leyland chassis. Roe-bodied Leyland Titan PD3/5 UWU 515 was photographed at Christ Church working the Moorends route, joint with Felix Motors and Premier. Severn's green and cream buses did not display fleet names at the time of this August 1962 picture. T. Severn & Sons Ltd was sold to South Yorkshire PTE on 30 March 1979. Vehicles remained licenced to the company until 24 August 1980. (Philip Wallis)

United Services was the collective fleet name used by three operators which shared operation of Doncaster to Wakefield and Wakefield to Hemsworth bus routes. All three fleets included ex-Ribble buses when photographed in 1962. (*Above*) Mrs Phyllis Bingley's (t/a W. R. and P. Bingley) 1951 'White Lady' East Lancs-bodied Leyland Titan PD2/3 DCK 221 was seen at Doncaster's Marshgate bus station. (Opposite *above*) Cooper Brothers 1949 Brush-bodied Leyland Titan PD2/3 CCK 646 was at Wakefield bus station. (*Opposite below*) W. Everett & Son's 1949 Brush-bodied PD2/3 CCK 653 was en route to Doncaster. Bingley acquired W. Everett & Son on 15 November 1969 and Cooper Brothers on 4 April 1977. Bingley's business was sold to Wellandfield Ltd, a subsidiary of West Yorkshire PTE, on 25 April 1977. (The Omnibus Society, Philip Wallis, The Omnibus Society)

Leeds Area

Major coach operator Barr & Wallace Arnold Trust Ltd controlled two small bus companies in the Leeds area. (*Above*) Farsley Omnibus Company Ltd operated between Pudsey and Tinshill, with routeing mostly just beyond the Leeds city boundary. 1950 Daimler CVD6 MUM 460, seen at Farsley, originally had a coach body but was rebodied as a high-bridge double-decker by Roe in 1956. (*Below*) Kippax & District Motor Company Ltd ran a route between Leeds and Ledston Luck. 1960 Roe-bodied Leyland Titan PD3/1 6237 UB was photographed at Leeds Central bus station in July 1962. Note the side panel advertisement for Wallace Arnold's car dealerships. Farsley Omnibus Company and Kippax & District's routes passed to Leeds City Transport on 31 March 1968. (The Omnibus Society, Philip Wallis)

Sheffield Area

T. D. Alexander moved from Scotland to Sheffield in 1947 where he built up a private hire and contract business trading as Greyhound. After returning to Scotland in 1960, to oversee his Scottish bus operations, his son Bob continued to run the Sheffield business. Greyhound in Sheffield was wound up in 1970 after which Bob continued to trade as Alexander's until retiring in 1987. DMO 686 was a former Thames Valley 1948 ECW-bodied Bristol L6A. (Thomas W. W. Knowles)

Booth & Fisher was based at Halfway and ran several bus routes into north Derbyshire and Nottinghamshire along with a route to Sheffield. 1953 Duple (Midland)-bodied Leyland Royal Tiger URA 601 was seen on arrival in Sheffield. Booth & Fisher (Motor Services) Ltd was acquired by South Yorkshire PTE on 13 February 1976. (J. S. Cockshott Archive)

A & C Wigmore Ltd of Dinnington operated a daily bus route into Sheffield. 1952 Metalcraft-bodied Leyland Royal Tiger PDH 515 was seen at Pond Street bus station. A & C Wigmore Ltd was acquired by Northern Bus Company Ltd, Dinnington, in autumn 1987. (Thomas W. W. Knowles)

Skipton Area

Ezra Laycock Ltd was an old established operator with a number of bus routes emanating from Barnoldswick. Laycock's presence around Skipton increased from 13 August 1961 with the acquisition of three routes from Silver Star Motor Services. Plaxton-bodied AEC Regal III RKU 221 was photographed at Skipton bus station working former Silver Star route to Carleton. RKU 221 and sister vehicle RKU 220 were put into service by original operator Gillards of Normanton in 1959, several years after production of Regal IIIs for the home market had ceased. This suggests that the chassis were either from a frustrated export order or old stock. Ezra Laycock Ltd was acquired by Pennine Motor Services on 31 July 1972. (Thomas W. W. Knowles)

Pennine Motor Services Ltd's main bus routes, including a lengthy service between Skipton and Lancaster, were jointly operated with Ribble. 1954 Roe-bodied Leyland Royal Tiger NWT 329 had its blind set for Pennine's base at Gargrave. Pennine Motor Services Ltd ceased trading on 16 May 2014. (The Omnibus Society)

York Area and East Yorkshire

Bailey's Bus Service Ltd operated daily bus routes from Pocklington to Stamford Bridge and to York. Duple Vista-bodied Bedford OBs were once the mainstay of many rural independents' fleets. Bailey's 1951 model AEN 63 was seen with another OB at York. Bailey's was sold to Ingleby's of York in 2007. Ingleby's was incorporated into K & J Logistics (the new York Pullman) in 2007. (The Omnibus Society)

P. W. Cherry & Son operated town services in Beverley. Former Southdown 1949 Windover-bodied Leyland Tiger PS1/1 HUF 270 was photographed at Beverley Market. Cherry Coaches was acquired by EYMS Ltd, a holding company controlling East Yorkshire Motor Services Ltd, on 5 April 1987. (Michael Dryhurst)

Connor & Graham Ltd operated a number of bus routes east of Hull. Former Southdown 1939 Beadle-bodied Leyland Titan TD5 FUF 236 was seen at Baker Street terminus in Hull. Connor & Graham's bus services passed to East Yorkshire on 1 March 1993. Coaching and contract activities followed in 1994. (J. S. Cockshott Archive)

A. H. & N. Giles (Imperial) of Barmby-in-the-Marsh ran a Wednesday and Saturday bus service into Goole. 1951 Plaxton-bodied Austin CXD NWB 500 was photographed in Ouse Street at Goole. (The Omnibus Society)

J. W. S. Moore (Favourite) of Cawood operated a Monday-only service into Selby – that town's market day. Remarkably, wartime Duple-utility-bodied Bedford OWB EWW 196, seen in Wide Street at Selby, remained in the fleet until 1964. (The Omnibus Society)

Reliance Motor Services operated bus service north from York to Helmsley. 1947 Barnaby-bodied Daimler CVD6 DDN 8 was photographed at St Leonard's Place in York. Reliance had been started by Edward Sheriff in the 1920s. Following his death in the 1960s the business was continued by his daughter and son-in-law, Carol and Ricard Shelton, who sold the business to John and Margaret Duff in November 1980. Reliance Motor Services Ltd continues to operate a fleet of sixteen buses from the Sutton-on-the Forest premises established by Edward Sheriff. (The Omnibus Society)

Ben Sketcher of Swinefleet operated a daily bus service between Goole and Crowle (in Lincolnshire). 1950 Plaxton-bodied Bedford OB GBE 848 was standing on layover in the centre of Ouse Street in Goole. Ben Sketcher's bus route was taken over by Lincolnshire RCC in May 1969. Sketcher continued with coaching activities. (The Omnibus Society)

John Howard Thornes of Bubwith operations included a bus route from Holme-on-Spalding Moor to Selby, taken over from York Pullman in May 1954. Former Maidstone & District 1951 Beadle-AEC NKT 348, rebuilt by M&D from pre-war AEC Regent components, was seen at Quay Street, Selby. Thornes Independent Ltd of Hemingbrough, near Selby, continues to run a successful bus and coach business. (The Omnibus Society)

Yorks & Lincs Road Services Ltd was based at Swinefleet and operated bus routes between Goole in Yorkshire and Gainsborough and Scunthorpe, both in Lincolnshire. 1950 Beccols-bodied Crossley SD42/7 JWW 676 was photographed in Ouse Street, Goole. Yorks & Lincs Road Services' bus routes were acquired by Lincolnshire RCC on 15 May 1967. (J. S. Cockshott Archive)